Original title:
Sapwood Scribbles

Copyright © 2025 Creative Arts Management OÜ
All rights reserved.

Author: Dante Kingsley
ISBN HARDBACK: 978-1-80567-398-9
ISBN PAPERBACK: 978-1-80567-697-3

Leafy scribbles and silent echoes

In the trees where squirrels play,
Leaves giggle in the sun's warm ray.
Branches twist in a dance so spry,
Whispers of laughter float on high.

Breezes carry secrets loud,
While shadows hide beneath a cloud.
Acorns fall with a thump so keen,
Turning serious moments to silly scenes.

From bark to verse in the wild

On bark, the stories start to hum,
Twirling tales with a plucky drum.
Unruly vines stretch out to tease,
And some wise owls snooze with ease.

Twigs tap dance on the forest floor,
Frogs croak lines as they leap and soar.
With a splash, the pond chimes in,
Echoing giggles, where fun begins.

Mapped in moss and petal ink

Mossy maps cover the forest's face,
Guiding dreams with a soft embrace.
Petals flutter, joining the plot,
In a garden of giggles, all tied in a knot.

Bumblebees buzz with comic flair,
As they waltz through sweet-scented air.
The petals blush, as they sway so light,
Tickled by rays of golden light.

The parchment of the ancient grove

In the grove where time stands still,
Ancient trees boast wisdom and thrill.
A parchment where stories intertwine,
Filled with whimsy, sunshine, and vine.

Rabbits write with their twitching nose,
Jotting down all the chuckles that rose.
Fungi giggle, while crickets trill,
In a world where laughter fits to fill.

Ink-stained nature's tales

In the forest where trees talk,
A squirrel's mischief, quite the mock.
With each scratch of a pen on bark,
They leave behind a humorous spark.

Bees buzz tales of a floral jam,
While ants plot grand, tiny bait-and-scam.
Nature's jesters, full of mirth,
Sketching fun upon the earth.

Lines drawn in the dirt

A stick in hand, a child sits low,
Sketching secrets for the world to know.
Jumping jacks and hopscotch news,
In dirt, the craziest tales ensues.

A wiggly worm becomes a knight,
Defending his fortress with all his might.
The sun giggles as shadows play,
Drawing laughter in a funny way.

The essence of the canopy's breath

Under leaves that chatter and sway,
The canopy whispers tales of play.
A breeze tickles the branches' song,
While acorns drop and laugh along.

A parrot's squawk, a punchline stray,
Echoes of mischief flutter and sway.
Nature's giggles rise and descend,
In every gust, where jokes won't end.

Memories imprinted by the wind

The wind carries scribbles on its wings,
Whispering secrets of funny things.
A paper plane takes flight, it seems,
Chasing dreams and tickling beams.

Old leaves cackle, sharing the lore,
Of dances beneath the trees galore.
With laughter etched in every swirl,
Nature's humor unfurls and twirls.

The sketch of the earth's heartbeat

In a world drawn in crayon, quite bright,
Trees likely giggle by day and by night.
A squirrel with glasses, a pencil in paw,
Sketching the earth with a giggly jaw.

Little ants wearing hats, strut and parade,
As grass blades cheer with a vibrant charade.
Doodles emerge from a puddle of paint,
While butterflies twirl like a boisterous saint.

Scribbles from the deep green

Amidst the green, laughter swirls in the air,
Frogs throw a party, with snacks everywhere.
A hedgehog's a DJ, spinning leaves to the beat,
While turtles dance funky on broad, grassy seats.

Bumblebees buzz in a jazzy, sweet tune,
While daisies nod gently, dancing to June.
Scribbles of nature, all covered in smiles,
Bring giggles and grins across all the miles.

A symphony in the forest's ink

The forest's an artist with plenty of flair,
Paints melodies bright, and fans everywhere.
Owls wearing bow ties sing songs in delight,
While raccoons clap paws, putting on quite the sight.

The wind starts to whistle, a comical sound,
As branches do a jig, twirling round and round.
Each note from the ferns, like whispers of cheer,
Creating a symphony that all creatures hear.

Versicles of the woodland's tales

In the heart of green, where laughter does bloom,
Bunnies weave stories amidst shady gloom.
With quills made of twigs, they scribble and write,
Chasing away clouds to let in the light.

Fables of flowers, all dressed up in cheer,
Each petal a tale of their woodland sphere.
In the ink of the sky, where dreams take their flight,
They giggle and whisper under stars at night.

Stories suspended in amber

In a jar full of beetles, they sit,
Fossils of chaos, never to quit.
Wiggly tales of a dragonfly's dance,
Caught in a bubble, lost in a trance.

Echoes of laughter from eons ago,
Tickled by sunlight and warmed by the glow.
Their giggles trapped in a resin-filled case,
Telling tall tales with a wink on their face.

The silence of old timber

The trees hold their breath, or so it seems,
Whispering secrets of childhood dreams.
Knots full of stories they struggle to tell,
Stifled by silence, but wishing them well.

Branches that creak with a chuckle or two,
Pondering life and what birds really knew.
They root for the squirrels, their nimble offense,
And giggle at woodpeckers, so full of pretense.

Poetic murmurs of the thicket

In the thicket, a rabbit wrote,
Verses of cabbage and chocolate float.
A poetry slam with a hedgehog crew,
Ruffles of leaves when the moles say boo!

Burrowing poets with ink-stained paws,
Murmurs of laughter, and playful applause.
A thistle's sharp critique, a daisy's sweet cheer,
Each line an adventure in frolic and fear.

Scribbles of shadows

Shadows dance lightly, like sketches in mist,
Doodling the corners the sun has missed.
A jumbled graffiti of laughter and fun,
Tracing the stories of games never done.

Whispers of giggles, they flicker and glide,
In the warm hues of evening, they skitter and hide.
The night holds its breath, urges them to play,
For shadows are scribbles that brighten the day.

Bark whispers in the breeze

The trees can't keep a secret, just a shout,
Their laughter ripples leaves, there's no doubt.
Branches bend with giggles, twirling with glee,
While squirrels steal the show, oh look at me!

In every creak and crack, stories collide,
Where birds throw a party, feathers wide.
Leaves dress up in hues, a fashion parade,
Nature's quirky humor, never to fade.

Inked rings of time's embrace

The old oak wears a crown of whispered lore,
Carving tales in rings, each a chuckle and roar.
Nature's comic saga, etched deep in bark,
A woodpecker's tap tap, a hilarious quark.

Seasons pass like punchlines, funny and bold,
While squirrels balance acorns, oh behold!
With every gust, the branches sway and tease,
Vintage portraits of laughter float on the breeze.

Twisted trails of memory

In the forest's embrace, memories twist and twine,
Like vines playing tricks, oh sweet design!
A raccoon's midnight snack, a face full of mud,
Laughter echoes softly, in a playful flood.

Each path holds a story, skip and stumble back,
Where mushrooms play dress-up, nature's fun hack.
With every glance around, new jokes unroll,
As shadows dance merrily, wild and whole.

Nature's whispered tales

In the rustling grass, a gossip whooshes by,
With whispers of mischief, oh me, oh my!
A ladybug winks, a hare hops along,
Dancing on petals, singing a song.

Frisky foxes plot their next escapade,
While frogs ribbit secrets in the cool glade.
Nature's own stand-up, comedy divine,
Where every leaf and critter plays their line.

Patterns traced in the woodland dusk

In the twilight's playful glow,
Leaves rustle, secrets blow.
Squirrels gossip, birds take flight,
Dancing shadows, pure delight.

Twigs twist, forming funny shapes,
Nature's laughter, no escape.
A frog croaks, quite a joke,
While mushrooms giggle, they provoke.

A rabbit hops with quirky grace,
Winks at me, a silly face.
The path ahead, a jumbled maze,
In this wood, we're lost in plays.

So come with me, let's roam and run,
In dusk where all is light and fun.
Patterns traced in every nook,
Nature's story, an open book.

The ink of the earth beneath my feet

The ground is soft, a squishy bed,
Where muddy footprints have been spread.
I slip and slide, a playful mess,
The earth beneath, a jester's dress.

With each step, a giggle's heard,
A worm hops up, "Hey there, nerd!"
Crickets chirp a silly tune,
As laughter swells beneath the moon.

My shoes now stained, a splatter show,
A canvas for the worms to flow.
Each color tells a joke or two,
In every step, the thrill is new.

So let's embrace this silly feat,
With ink of earth beneath our feet.
A muddy dance, both bright and sweet,
In this laughter, we're complete!

Soft murmurs of a verdant canvas

Whispers weave through leaf and vine,
Painted greens in a playful line.
The flowers chuckle, petals sway,
A fine art class at break of day.

Giggling bumblebees at play,
Buzzing tunes that lead astray.
Dandelions puff, they conspire,
To tickle noses, fuel desires.

Tall trees bend, their branches bow,
In this lush realm, I take a vow.
To dance with weeds, embrace each sprout,
In nature's joy, let laughter out.

Canvas bright, a tapestry,
In soft murmurs, wild and free.
Let's twirl among this verdant dream,
In every corner, laughter gleams.

An ode to the timbered horizon

A horizon clad in wood and cheer,
Nature's theater, crystal clear.
Each tree a character, wise and bold,
Telling tales that never get old.

The sun winks down, a playful spark,
In shadows deep, I'm free to mark.
With owls that hoot and critters that tease,
The timbered line sings with glee and ease.

Chirps and creaks, the woodlands hum,
Every echo feels like fun.
Let's scale the heights, feel the breeze,
In every giggle, find our keys.

So raise a cheer to this vast view,
Timbered hues of every hue.
An ode to joy in every tree,
Where laughter rings eternally.

Portraits of the Silent Grove

In the quiet woods, trees wear frowns,
Squirrels gossip in their leafy crowns.
Mice play cards under moonlit beams,
While owls swap tales of their wild dreams.

Branches dance, a wobbly ballet,
Barking dogs join in the fray.
A hedgehog spins on a little wheel,
Singing songs of a squeaky peel.

But the best is a crow in a bow tie,
Cracking jokes as the days float by.
The trees chuckle, their laughter bold,
As new silly stories start to unfold.

The Language of Leaves

Leaves whisper secrets in a breeze,
Tickling branches, oh how they tease!
A maple says, 'Hey, look at my dance!'
While oaks roll their eyes at a squirrel's prance.

Vines twist up in a giddy race,
Buds blush bright in their sunny grace.
Beneath the boughs, a rabbit sneezes,
And all around, the laughter eases.

Sometimes a nut drops with a thud,
Stirring up the fallen flood.
But the trees just sway, with winks and grins,
In a chat about which bird wins.

Memoirs of the Wooden Heart

Old stumps tell tales of days gone by,
Of chipmunks prancing and clouds that sigh.
A knot in the trunk shares its deep lore,
As ants march proudly on a wooden floor.

A woodpecker knocks with a humorous beat,
While frogs practice leaps near the old tree's feet.
Collecting mischief, the bark's cracked wide,
Hiding giggles in every side.

'Knotty problems!' the trees all laugh,
As they recount their silly craft.
In the forest's heart, joy's the refrain,
True tales of laughter, again and again.

Traces of Time in Timber

Once a sapling, I grew so tall,
Hiding dreams in my leafy hall.
With time-worn bark, I wear my tales,
Of fuzzy bees and windy gales.

Wrinkles show in each sturdy limb,
The stories of storms in a playful whim.
Twirling acorns kick up dirt,
As critters play where the sunlight flirts.

From the laughter of crows to a wise old bee,
Every creak in my frame has a history.
The winds weave their yarns, silly and bright,
In my wooden heart, a world of delight.

Softly Written in Nature's Hand

Leaves giggle on the breeze,
Squirrels dance in the trees.
Acorns fall like tiny bombs,
Nature's chaos, sweetly calms.

Amidst the roots, a worm spins tales,
About the jesters in the gales.
Mushrooms wear their polka dots,
Though some just think it's all for naught.

Clouds hang low, a fluffy crowd,
Whispers loud, though not too proud.
Caterpillars drawing schemes,
On behalf of fast-pacing dreams.

Doodles of a Dappled Sun

The sun spills paint across the land,
Tickling blossoms, oh so grand.
Bees buzzing out their funny tunes,
While the grass tries on new hues.

A butterfly in pajamas flies,
Chasing shadows 'neath the skies.
Laughter echoes, a gentle jest,
As critters play in nature's quest.

Sunbeams stretch like silly strings,
Wrapping branches as joy sings.
Each ripple in the water's face,
Holds bubbles of a wild embrace.

Chronicles of the Canopy

In the canopy, whispers play,
As branches share a tale each day.
A woodpecker's knock is a secret code,
While squirrels plan their acorn road.

Ferns twirl, trying to impress,
With their fronds, a fancy dress.
Raccoons dip their paws in paint,
Creating art, oh what a saint!

The wise old owl, with spectacles near,
Calls out jokes that we all hear.
Every twinkling star a wink,
In the tree's great, leafy sink.

The Bark Beneath My Fingertips

Beneath my touch, the bark can laugh,
Telling tales of the forest's path.
Rough and ready, its stories unfold,
In twists and turns of ages old.

A family of ants makes a parade,
While the sun hides, in the shade.
Woodlice shuffle, wearing frowns,
As leaves drop like tiny clowns.

Moss giggles as I step near,
Whispering secrets for me to hear.
Every tree, a smile it flips,
In the forest's funny scripts.

The melody of foliage's verse

Leaves dance to a rustling beat,
Whispering tunes on branches sweet.
Squirrels take the stage, oh so spry,
In leafy hats, they leap and fly.

A woodpecker's tap, a funny drum,
Echoes through the woods, here they come!
Chirping birds break into song,
Nature's choir sings all day long.

Breezes tickle the trembling trees,
Laughter floats on the playful breeze.
With twirling vines and playful sprout,
Nature's jesters dance about.

In this forest, joy runs free,
Silly antics for all to see.
Each leaf tells a story, grins wide,
In the funny foliage's ride.

Scribbled dreams in the boughs

Branches stretch, like kids at play,
Swinging high in the bright sun's ray.
Clouds drift by, painting the blue,
While birds make wishes, funny and few.

Inky shadows paint the ground,
As giggles of leaves swirl all around.
A raccoon prances, stealing a snack,
With a wink and a hop, no turning back.

The sun doodles rays on a leafy sheet,
Drawing funny faces, so silly and sweet.
Each twig a pencil, each bough a page,
In sketchy tales, the forest's stage.

Night unfolds, stars start to shine,
Drawing patterns that feel just fine.
In the quiet, dreams take flight,
Scribbled tales in the soft moonlight.

Twilight's tapestry of thoughts

As day whispers its last goodnight,
Colors blend, a glorious sight.
Leaves chuckle, feeling quite proud,
Wearing dusk like a cozy shroud.

Fireflies twinkle, a playful jest,
While crickets chirp, they know best.
The moon joins in, with a gleeful grin,
To weave stories, let the fun begin.

Branches bend low, secrets they share,
Chasing shadows without a care.
Rustling papers of whispers past,
A funny dance, forever to last.

In twilight's glow, laughter sings,
The forest turns to lively things.
A tapestry rich, woven with cheer,
Nature's humor draws us near.

Whims of nature's delicate hand

Petals flutter in soft ballet,
Twisting, twirling, come what may.
A playful breeze, a gentle tease,
Cartwheeling leaves with the utmost ease.

Ants parade with tiny crowns,
Marching straight through muddy towns.
Each little step, a funny flair,
In nature's capers, they dance with care.

Grass blades giggle, tickling toes,
While ladybugs strike funny poses.
With polka-dot dresses and tiny hats,
They prance about, oh imagine that!

Nature whispers, jokes abound,
In her realms, joy can be found.
With every whim and a little chance,
Life grows brighter in this dance.

Poetry carved in fallen leaves

Leaves dance in the breeze, so bold,
Each one a story, funny and old.
A squirrel reads poems, perched on a branch,
As acorns giggle in a nutty dance.

Cradled in sunbeams, the shadows take flight,
Pinecones chuckle, oh what a sight!
They share their rhymes, in nature's own play,
While branches nod off, what a lazy day!

Footprints wander on paths of delight,
As critters steal snacks in the soft twilight.
Each rustle brings laughter, a giggling sound,
In the heart of the woods, joy can be found.

Oh, the fallen leaves, what a comedic stage,
Nature's monologues, truly engage!
As shadows sway, and the sun starts to tease,
Life's leaf-strewn poems bring smiles, if you please!

The woodlands' lyrical foliage

In a grove where the giggles grow tall,
Trees wear their leaves like a leafy shawl.
The wind writes sonnets, with a cheeky twist,
Beneath the canopies, no fun's ever missed.

Mushrooms pop up, with tops like a hat,
Singing sweet pipers, imagine that!
Birds crack jokes perched high in their choir,
While bushes blush under tales they inspire.

Beneath the soft boughs, there's mischief galore,
Rabbits recount tales of past woodland lore.
The flowers giggle, their petals all bright,
In this leafy theater, everything's light.

The moon winks down, setting stars all aglow,
As nighttime jam sessions begin, oh so slow.
With giggles in the air, and joy on the stage,
The woodlands hum tunes, resonating with age!

Fragments of light in a forest's embrace

Sunbeams tickle the leaves, oh what a sight,
Casting shadows that giggle, dazzling and bright.
A bunny recites, with a hop and a twirl,
As dandelion wishes begin to unfurl.

The forest hums softly, a tune from the past,
With echoes of laughter in every blast.
Whispers of wind play hide and seek,
While merry old trees nod with a creak.

Glowworms glimmer, their lights like a spark,
Guiding lost shoes that were left in the dark.
Mushrooms play poker on a mossy old log,
While shadows and moonbeams melt in the fog.

In nature's embrace, where fun never fades,
Each rustle and laugh form the sweetest cascades.
So dance in this light, let your worries erase,
For fragments of joy fill this magical place!

Jotting down whispers of the earth

Listen closely, the earth tells a joke,
In the rippling brook, where the shy fish poke.
Branches snicker softly, leaves share their dreams,
While crickets compose a chorus, it seems.

Grass blades chuckle, so green and spry,
As playful breezes flit and fly.
A fox in a hat struts down the lane,
Confounding the walkers with quirks in the grain.

Nature's sly giggles tangle in thorns,
While daisies act wise in their countless adorns.
The sly whisperings echo, exciting the lore,
As pine needles ruffle like laughs from before.

So grab your notepad, and jot down the sights,
Of laughter in gravel, and joy on the nights.
For whispers of earth are a rollicking glee,
Inviting us all to dance merrily!

The language of living trees

Whispering leaves in the breeze,
Mocking the squirrels and their tease.
Gnarled branches twist and sway,
Telling tales in their own way.

Roots tangled like feet in a race,
Trees gossiping at a slow pace.
Laughter echoes through the bark,
While owls chuckle after dark.

Fungi giggle in their own style,
Waving at passersby with a smile.
Bouncing acorns drop with a thud,
Creating a trunk-sized laugh flood.

So join the dance in the green,
Where nature bustles, a rolling scene.
Each bough a jester, each trunk a clown,
In this leafy circus, let's not frown.

Shadows in the woodland heart

Shadows play on the forest floor,
Creating stories we can't ignore.
A raccoon slips with a comical flair,
While deer giggle without a care.

Beneath the boughs, the sunlight stutters,
As a breeze tickles the leaves like butters.
Mice in bowties hold their own show,
In a game of hide and seek, oh so slow.

The wind whispers jokes in the trees,
Like a stand-up set, bringing you to your knees.
Branches shake, the owls roll their eyes,
As snickers erupt from the woodland skies.

Each shadow dances, a cheeky tease,
Inviting all to join the trees.
In this comedy club of nature's art,
The woodland chuckles in its heart.

Beneath the canopy's script

Under the canopy, stories unwind,
With laughter woven and joy intertwined.
Acorns gossip with a playful cheer,
As the squirrels strut, showing off their gear.

With each rustle, the leaves crack a joke,
While damp earth claps in a jovial cloak.
Mushrooms dance in a burst of glee,
As shadows twist in a woodland spree.

A breeze weaves tales like a cunning bard,
Tickling the trunks, leaving them charred.
Cardinals chuckle, their wings taking flight,
While the brook chuckles under the moonlight.

So gather 'round this nature's script,
Where fun and folly are tightly gripped.
Each twig a word, each branch a rhyme,
In this living poem, we laugh every time.

Etchings of the forest floor

Etched in mud, a silly surprise,
Footprints lead to where laughter lies.
A critter rolls down a sloping hill,
Creating giggles, a joyful thrill.

The moss carpets like a soft green tease,
Where beetles march, dancing with ease.
Fallen leaves act as confetti in fall,
Celebrating the clumps of critters that crawl.

Nuts and berries join the fiesta loud,
Nature's munchies, gathering a crowd.
Hooting owls take the stage at night,
With shadows playing under soft moonlight.

Each element's a unique funny score,
In the grand concert of the forest floor.
So twirl and tumble, let laughter roar,
In this woodland giggle, forevermore.

Whispers of the Bark

In the forest where whispers play,
Bark giggles softly, come what may.
Squirrels debate, acorns in hand,
While ants march by, forming a band.

Trees wear hats made of leaves so bright,
They dance in the breeze, what a sight!
Mushrooms chuckle, oh what a dream,
A party of nature, or so it seems.

The owls hoot jokes from high up above,
As branches sway with a hint of love.
A raccoon juggles, oh what a spree,
In this woody world, wild and free.

So listen closely, to nature's cheer,
In the whispers of bark, laughter draws near.

Echoes in the Grain

The wood grain tells tales of old,
Of splinters and knots, some funny and bold.
A come-and-go through the ages,
With laughter echoing through history's pages.

A squirrel once sat atop a tall throne,
On a branch of oak, all alone.
He crafted a crown from crisp autumn leaves,
Proclaimed himself king – oh how he weaves!

The woodpecker drums a comical beat,
As ants tap dance, nimble on their feet.
Echoes in grain, a funny how-to,
Garden of giggles, those woodlands woo.

With knots like faces, and rings like smiles,
Nature's humor stretches miles and miles.

Between the Rings

In the life of a tree, there's so much glee,
Between the rings is where jokes run free.
A joke may be hidden in each little space,
As the bark cracks a grin, it dons a new face.

A bumblebee buzzed with a witty pun,
In the grand forest, laughter is spun.
Said the beetle, "Why do trees never get lost?"
"Because they always know how much it costs!"

A parrot squawks with a colorful joke,
The leaves all tremble, it's quite a hoax!
Wily and wise, the creatures convene,
To share all the banter that's fit for a scene.

Together they laugh, crafting stories so fine,
In the rings of a tree, nature's design.

The Tender Veins of Forests

The tender veins of woods are a laugh,
Frogs croak out jokes, what a joyful path!
As flowers gossip in hues so bright,
The sun winks down, oh what a delight!

A beaver jokes, "I'm building a dam,
But first, I need a sandwich – I'm quite the ham!"
The river chuckles, with ripples so clear,
While the moon whispers secrets, never near.

With shadows that dance, each part has a role,
In the forest's play, they all fill a hole.
Critters unite, sharing tales of mirth,
In the veins of the forest, life knows its worth.

So gather 'round nature, where humor is king,
In this lively theatre, let your heart sing!

Roots entwined in poetic lines

In the garden where giggles grow,
Trees tickle each other, you know.
With branches that dance like silly strings,
They whisper of all the funny things.

Leaves burst with laughter, oh what a sight,
A squirrel in a suit takes off in flight.
Roots twist in rhythm, a comical cheer,
Nature's own jesters are always near.

With every rustle, a new joke is spun,
In this tangled mess, we just can't outrun.
A snail in a hat starts a slow-motion race,
While mushrooms chuckle, finding their place.

Here under the canopy, mischief takes flight,
Where shadows and sunlight share pure delight.
So tiptoe through these humor-filled woods,
With puns in your pocket—head to the hoods!

Traces of the woodland muse

Whispers of whimsy drift through the trees,
A fox in a bowtie, if you please.
Each twig tells a tale with a wink and a grin,
Of sap-sipping squirrels breaking their spin.

Moss carpets the path where giggles reside,
A butterfly sings, it can't be denied.
Nature's a canvas where laughter's the hue,
Each leaf a brushstroke, it's funny but true!

A deer drops a joke, and the owls take note,
As the rabbits all laugh, and the night comes afloat.
In this woodland wonder, each glance draws a smile,
Adventure unfolds, let's stay for a while!

With mushrooms in chequered hats and capes,
The forest is filled with joyous shapes.
So dance with the shadows, let your spirit muse,
In this lively haven where silliness brews!

Words woven in wooden veins

In the heart of the forest, whispers align,
Branches exchange secrets, all by design.
Words flow like sap through the fibers of cheer,
An echo of laughter that everyone hears.

Woodpeckers tap a tune on the tree,
Creating a symphony, as happy as can be.
With every knock-knock, a giggle escapes,
As nature unfolds all its funniest shapes.

A raccoon wears glasses, quite stylish indeed,
While the hedgehogs read books, planting the seed.
Stories unfurl in a whimsical way,
As laughter and joy come to play every day.

Tangled vines twist like jests in the air,
Jokes shared with critters without a care.
Words woven in bark, in leaf, and in wind,
Nature's tapestry where humor's all pinned!

Fragments of the earth's heartbeat

In the rhythm of roots, a chuckle takes flight,
With each gentle thump, nature's laughter ignites.
The earth's heart is playful, a jester at play,
As sunlight sneaks in to brighten the day.

A turtle winks slyly, he knows all the jokes,
While the shadows of trees come to life with folks.
With giggles and grins, the flowers all sway,
In this fragrant ballet, they dance and they play.

Ripples of humor spread wide like a stream,
As critters collide in a whimsical dream.
Roots reach out in laughter, embracing the fun,
With each hearty pulse, the woodland is spun.

So listen quite closely, to what nature shares,
In fragments of laughter, all it declares.
The heart of the earth beats a rhythm so sweet,
Join in with the joy; let your laughter repeat!

Pencils made of twigs and dreams

In a forest of jolly dreams,
Twigs scribble on sunlit beams.
They dance and prance, what a sight,
Drawing giggles, taking flight.

With caps of acorns, sharp and neat,
They sketch out paths for tiny feet.
Each line a laugh, a twist, a shout,
In woodland classes, there's no doubt.

Chasing squirrels, dodging rain,
They write of joy, they write of gain.
Peeking through branches, grinning wide,
Those playful tools, with nature, abide.

Whispers of dreams in every stroke,
These twigs are more than simple folk.
With jests and jibes, they color fate,
Oh what a world they create!

The heartbeats of ancient oaks

Listen close, oh can you hear?
The thumping tales of yesteryear.
Oaks chuckle, each ring a tale,
Of winds and storms, and ships that sail.

Leaves clap hands in sunlit glee,
Beating rhythms, wild and free.
Branches sway, they groove and swing,
As ancient laughter starts to sing.

Roots beneath, in whispers speak,
Sharing secrets, oh so sleek.
They tickle thoughts from ground to sky,
In this forest, nobody's shy.

So let us dance beneath their shade,
With every beat, a joke is laid.
Join the fun, let's twirl about,
In heartbeats of oaks, joy's no doubt!

Musings between the leaves

Underneath the leafy roof,
Squirrels muse, with truth aloof.
They laugh in whispers, share a grin,
While dandelions join in, spin!

Stories flutter, rustle bright,
As breezes blow, they take to flight.
Each leaf a page, a funny find,
With giggles rooted in the mind.

Worms compose their earthy rhymes,
While worms tap dance in leafy climes.
In this realm of green delight,
Nature's jesters, all in sight.

So pause a while, take it in,
Where laughter grows and dreams begin.
In every rustle, hear a shout,
Musings abound without a doubt!

Verses from the roots of wisdom

Deep in the soil, wisdom grows,
Roots whisper secrets that nobody knows.
With playful quips and earthy sass,
They crack up the stones, make the lost grass.

Their stories wriggle, shake, and laugh,
Weaving tales of the tallest staff.
Each twist and turn, a funny clue,
Of how old trees gained life anew.

From mossy banks to tangled vines,
Wisdom chuckles in grand designs.
With giggly grubs and cheeky sprouts,
Nature's humor is what it's about.

So gather 'round, lend an ear,
To silly roots that revere cheer.
With each old tale, a grin reborn,
In the wisdom of roots, new joys adorn!

Fleeting Thoughts in Wood Grain

A squirrel's joke on a swirling breeze,
Leaves giggle as they dance with ease.
Bark begins to chuckle, quite absurd,
As acorns roll by, their laughter stirred.

Sunlight tickles branches overhead,
Whispers float where the woodpecker fed.
In the shade, a beetle starts to rhyme,
While shadows play a game with time.

Rainy clouds drop jokes from afar,
As puddles form a laughing reservoir.
A toad croaks the punchline, so spry,
While ants line up for a comedy fry.

The twigs exchange tales, with a wink,
Moss adds a twist, as cabbage will stink.
There's humor in every sapling's grin,
In the woodland world, where laughs begin.

Artwork of the Arboreal

Among the branches, a brush takes flight,
Colorful splashes splatter, what a sight!
Caterpillars lounge in their artful phase,
While butterflies flaunt at the end of the rays.

Twigs become brushes, leaves add the flair,
Sticks play the drums, oh what a fair!
Nature's palette—funny and bright,
A symphony of giggles in daytime light.

Raccoons tag trees with a mischievous hand,
Scribbling tales as they dance through the land.
Flowers get painted with laughter and glee,
As wind carries giggles from tree to tree.

In the trunk's deep grooves, secrets unfold,
Stories of squirrels and acorns bold.
Through bark and through blossom, good times align,
Each frame a funny twist, each leaf a sign.

Tales Woven in Twigs

Twine and tree knots spin a quirky yarn,
With each little twist, the laughter is born.
Squirrels are storytellers, witty and spry,
Their anecdotes fly as they leap and fly.

Nuts tell of adventures in their cozy shell,
While shadows of owls sip on storytelling swell.
The roots hum a tune of jigs and surprises,
Branching out into giggles, where joy never dies.

A bunny hops in, joins the jamboree,
With hops that crack jokes like branches on spree.
Through valleys of whispers, the stories will weave,
Creating a tapestry you wouldn't believe.

In thickets of laughter, the night starts to sing,
Crickets strum melodies, making hearts swing.
With twigs as our quills, we write in the air,
Tales of the woods, oh, how wondrously rare!

Lines Etched in Nature's Spine

On the bark of a tree, a storyline grows,
With every carved line, the laughter flows.
A spider spins giggles in shimmering thread,
As wood rats rehearse their wisecrack ahead.

Branches bend low, with whispers so fine,
While nuts tell their secrets in curves and in twine.
Birch trees break into song, laughter so bright,
As the sun dips low, painting day into night.

Gnarled roots chuckle at the snickers of time,
As breezes of jokes round every old rhyme.
Wings flutter softly, a punchline in flight,
As critters convene for the wood's open mic.

Nature's own storybook, pages of glee,
Written in silence, for you and for me.
With every fresh chapter, we're drawn deeper in,
In the spine of the trees, where the laughter will spin.

Nature's quiet sonnet

In the forest where the trees giggle,
Leaves rustle softly, a gentle wiggle.
Squirrels barter nuts with frantic grace,
As the owl winks, hiding his face.

Bark beetles dance on wood with flair,
Whispers of secrets tickle the air.
A spider spins jokes on a silken thread,
While the mice convene and share their bread.

The brook chuckles as it flows along,
Bubbling up laughter in its song.
Nature's humor, a whimsical spree,
Tickling every branch, every glee.

In this quiet wood, there's mirth abound,
In every nook, wit can be found.
So listen closely to the playful breeze,
Nature's secrets shared with ease.

Scribbles of the sylvan sigh

Trees etch stories on their bark,
Sketching shadows deep and dark.
With a cheeky grin, the wind does tease,
Whispering tales through the leaves and trees.

An ant in a tux, oh so dapper,
Marches past, quite the chapper.
While butterflies giggle, flit and swerve,
In this lively dance, they serve and curve.

A frog croaks puns, quite absurd,
While the birds tweet, chirping the word.
In the meadow where the daisies sway,
Nature's jesters come out to play.

So take a moment, pause and look,
At the laughter written, like a book.
In every rustle, in every sight,
The woodland whispers with pure delight.

Chronicles of the greenwood

In the glade where giggles grow,
The sunbeams join in a glowing show.
Mushrooms wear hats, all spruced and neat,
As rabbits dodge around on tiny feet.

A deer cracks jokes with the passing breeze,
Tickling ferns, provoking a tease.
While the sunflowers nod, oh so spry,
Chatting away with a friendly sigh.

The shadows dance, shifting with glee,
An orchestra played by nature, you see.
Each rustle a laugh, every flutter a jest,
In the chronicles told by every quest.

Gather 'round and listen well,
For in greenwood tales, laughter dwells.
Nature's humor, witty and spry,
Invites us all to join and fly.

Logs that speak in the twilight

In twilight's glow, the logs convene,
Charming stories, oh, so serene.
With the toads as poets, croaking late,
While the fireflies dance, sealing their fate.

The saplings giggle, their branches sway,
Eager to share what they have to say.
Mischief abounds in the cooling light,
While shadows stretch, igniting the night.

A wise old log recounts his travels,
Through storms and sunny, joyous marvels.
Raccoons roll their eyes, full of swagger,
Telling tall tales, with a playful swagger.

So listen close as darkness creeps,
For the woodland secrets, it gently keeps.
In every whisper, and every spark,
The logs hold laughter in the deepening dark.

Reflections in Resin

In a tree's embrace, a squirrel plays,
Chasing dreams in this leafy maze.
He pauses to ponder, with eyes so wide,
What happened to nuts that he tried to hide?

With sap like glue, he sticks to the bark,
Telling tall tales that leave quite a mark.
The owls roll their eyes, with a wink and a nudge,
As he speaks of a treasure he'll never judge.

A twigged-up dance, a wobbly spin,
"Watch me, oh friends, let the fun begin!"
But round and around, he leads a parade,
While the sun sets low, and night starts to invade.

As laughter rings through the woodsy air,
Even the trees can't help but stare.
In shiny resin, all tales are sealed,
Of this funny rodent, forever revealed.

A Forest's Diary

Dear Diary, today, I saw quite the sight,
A raccoon in boots, what a curious plight!
He danced with the shadows, a whimsical flair,
Said he was late for a glamorous affair.

Then came the fox, in his newest cap,
With stories of mischief that made the trees clap.
Each branch chimed in with a rustling cheer,
While the frogs croaked softly, enjoying the leer.

A woodpecker tapped out some beats on a log,
As a band of ants formed a tiny prologue.
With rhythms and laughs ringing through every nook,
Even the grumpy old owl took a look.

So here I will write, as the day fades away,
Of antics and giggles in leafy ballet.
The forest, my friend, a stage so divine,
Where laughter and joy intertwine like a vine.

The Poetry of the Timbered Voice

A tree stood tall, with a trunk so round,
Claiming to be the wisest around.
"Listen close, little critters," he'd croon,
"I've got stories to share 'neath the brightening moon."

But as he spun tales of decades gone past,
A beetle marched by, and he giggled quite fast.
"Old tree, you're a riot! You crack me up,"
As the branches shook gently, full of good luck.

With rings made of laughter, each layer a jest,
His bark held secrets—some silly, some blessed.
The creatures all gathered, in twirls and in spins,
Joining the rhythms as the poetry begins.

So here's to the wood that tells its own tales,
Of whimsical creatures in whimsical trails.
A forest of giggles, a choir of fun,
In the heart of the woods, where laughter's begun.

Fragments of the Forest Floor

Scattered about are bits and pieces,
A acorn's forlorn, a gingerbread thesis.
Mushrooms don hats, in colors so bright,
As they gossip and giggle in soft morning light.

Leaves whisper secrets, as breezes collide,
With hues of adventure, they take in their stride.
A turtle in slippers, oh what a sight,
Races the rabbit, both full of delight.

The grass tickles toes with a playful embrace,
While ants, with their sandwiches, dash in a race.
"Mind the mushrooms! They're sprightly today,"
They muddle and tumble, all in good play.

As dusk draws near, with a softening glow,
The forest hums softly, in rhythms they know.
Fragments unite, in love and in jest,
This woodsy escapade is surely the best!

Sketches Beneath the Canopy

Underneath the leafy shade,
Trees tell jokes in their own way.
Branches twist like dancers there,
Whispering secrets as they sway.

Squirrels sketch with nimble paws,
Drawing acorns on the breeze.
Nature giggles, without pause,
A canvas full of chuckling trees.

Sunbeams laugh through forest lanes,
Painting shadows, wild and free.
Each twig tells of silly gains,
While birds compose a melody.

So grab a seat, enjoy the show,
The woodland's antics never cease.
A gallery where laughter grows,
In every rustle, there's a tease.

Silhouettes of a Timber Tale

In the woods, the shadows play,
Sketching figures day by day.
An owl wears a scholar's hat,
While raccoons debate on that!

Bobbing branches seem to sway,
In rhythm with the birds' ballet.
Each leaf is a script unread,
Where tales of mischief are widespread.

A faint log logs a joke or two,
As mushrooms giggle in their crew.
Bark scratches out a funny line,
And moss grows green with humor's vine.

The trees chuckle with every breeze,
Holding stories meant to tease.
In the forest, joy distills,
On silhouettes, life spills.

Ink of the Ancients

With every sap drop, stories flow,
Old trees write what they know.
Bark's the page, roots the quill,
Nature's humor, ever still.

A bear in glasses, finds his books,
While chipmunks sneak in guilty looks.
Wandering winds carry the jest,
Of woodland critters, quite impressed.

Mushrooms posture, aiming for fame,
Underneath a big old name.
Fun flows through the ancient ink,
Where logs sip tea, and softly wink.

Night falls, and the stories grow,
With laughter echoing, soft and low.
Planting joy with every phase,
Nature's quirks, a funny craze.

Nature's Drafts of Life

Here's a draft from nature's pen,
Filled with giggles now and then.
Frogs croak out a catchy rhymes,
While ants march on in silly lines.

Bees buzz jokes as they zoom by,
Though pollen masks their hearty cry.
Each flower bursts with laughter loud,
Joining in with every crowd.

The brook babbles quirky tales,
Of fish that wore their own set tails.
Bubbles burst with comic flair,
A playhouse where all creatures share.

The canvas spreads, the colors bloom,
In nature's drafts, there's room for doom.
But laughter floods like morning light,
In every leaf, a pure delight.

Stories held in timber's grip

In knots and twists, the tales unwind,
With whispers, the aged trees remind.
Squirrels chatter, holding court on high,
   While branches wave to passersby.

A lumberjack's hat, so full of dreams,
Held tight with laughter, bursting seams.
The rings reveal the years of cheer,
   In every slice, a story's seer.

Woodpeckers tap like drums of old,
   Echoing secrets, bold yet told.
With every thump, a joke does land,
In the heart of timber, life is grand.

The shade of leaves, a playground vast,
Where acorns dance in shadowed cast.
Each gnarled root a throne to claim,
In bark's embrace, we join the game.

Under the shade of reverent boughs

Beneath the canopy, the secrets lie,
With giggles hidden from the sky.
Leaves rustle softly, a playful tease,
While squirrels leap with utmost ease.

In this realm of green, we jest and jibe,
As nature crafts our playful tribe.
Each twig a wand, casting spells so bright,
Turns the mundane into pure delight.

Wooden chairs with stories glued,
Who knew that logs could give such mood?
With splinters sharp, but laughter round,
In nature's lap, our joy is found.

The sunbeams filter through the trees,
Filling our hearts with light breeze.
Each branch a friend, each root a call,
Under the boughs, we laugh through it all.

The verses of a thousand seasons

Seasons dance in vibrant hues,
Sprightly leaves bring forth new views.
Woodland tales from ages past,
In every ring, the shadows cast.

Caterpillars turn with a swish,
While squirrels plot their nutty wish.
Echoes linger, both grand and small,
In every creak, a former thrall.

The trees hum tunes of joy and cheer,
With every breeze, they draw us near.
Nature's poets, branches sway,
In wood and leaf, the world's ballet.

From winter's gloom to summer's bliss,
A story spun with every kiss.
These verses thrived through rain and shine,
In the heart of nature, tales intertwine.

In the language of the living wood

Bark speaks softly, a sage so wise,
With nature's charm, our spirits rise.
In every knot, a riddle lies,
Where laughter nestled, never dies.

From acorn to oak, the journey's bright,
Confessions whispered in the night.
The trunk stands sturdy, proud and bold,
As secrets bloom, like buds of gold.

Birds chirp gossip, sharing tea,
Under the shade, they all agree.
Every leaf a note in the script,
In the wood's language, joy is dipped.

And when the winds begin to play,
The boughs shake hands in a merry sway.
With each tickle of the playful breeze,
The living wood invites us, "Please!"

Petals of the Past

In the garden where ducks play,
Old flip-flops drove the bugs away.
A cat in a hat did pirouettes,
As flowers laughed at old man's pets.

Squirrels practiced their ballet,
While daisies dreamed of a cabaret.
The sun wore sunglasses bright,
As shadows danced into the night.

Bees played tag among the pots,
While ants huddled in tiny knots.
A snail in a tie drew a crowd,
As petals swayed and laughed out loud.

The breeze whispered silly puns,
Amusing trees and their tiny sons.
With every giggle, blooms were cast,
In memories bright—the petals last.

Vignettes of Woodland Whimsy

A raccoon wore a wizard's hat,
Conjuring spells, or so they spat.
The chipmunks chuckled, oh what fun,
As mushrooms cheered, 'Let's eat the sun!'

Frogs croaked tunes to the half-moon,
While owls rolled dice at high noon.
Each tree became a jolly clown,
As twigs threw confetti all around.

Bunnies plotted a silly race,
Hop, hop, hop—a furry chase!
While ladybugs kept score with glee,
Dreaming of gold in their tiny spree.

A porcupine danced, prickles a-glow,
Twirling around in a vibrant show.
With laughter echoed in the glade,
Whimsy flourished, never to fade.

The Canvas of Conifers

In a forest of green, pine trees stood,
Painting smiles like only they could.
With limbs stretched wide, they took a bow,
Dressing up for a hoedown wow!

Squirrels crafted a masterpiece,
With acorn paints, they never cease.
Each brushstroke caused the birds to sing,
Nature's art, a merry fling.

A woodpecker tapped the rhythm tight,
While mushrooms glowed in the soft moonlight.
Hares in jeans brought snacks to share,
As artists laughed without a care.

Closet elves joined the vibrant spree,
With tape and brushes, it's pure glee.
Together, they wove a playful trance,
In the canvas of trees, they pranced.

Sonnet of the Sylvan Shadows

In twilight's glow, the shadows prance,
A tap-dancing fox leads the merry dance.
While trees chuckle in a whispering plight,
As owls play cards under the starry night.

Bunnies giggle, dressed in swanky gear,
Debating if carrots are better than beer.
The crickets chirp a tune so spry,
While fireflies wink beneath the sky.

A hedgehog serenades the moon so bright,
As starlit tails weave shadows of light.
The forest hums with stories to tell,
Where laughter echoes, and all is well.

Each leaf a giggle, each root a rhyme,
In this dreamy realm, they play with time.
With every chuckle, the night unfolds,
In sylvan shadows, pure fun beholds.

The rhythm of the forest floor

Tap dancing ants march in a line,
They practice their moves, quite divine.
Wiggles and giggles bounce all around,
As mushrooms pop off the muddy ground.

Squirrels hold parties on branches high,
With acorn hats, they reach for the sky.
Raccoons in tuxedos join in the fun,
While rabbits do flips, oh what a run!

Even the ferns start to sway and groove,
To the beat of the leaves, they all start to move.
A conga line forms among the trees,
Nature's own disco, a sight to please.

All creatures laugh, the forest ignites,
With joy and laughter under moonlit nights.
The rhythm continues, no signs slow down,
For it's a wild party in woodland's crown.

Whispers caught in branches' dance

Branches chat gossip, oh what a tease,
"Did you hear that? Just a buzz in the breeze!"
Leaves giggle softly, swaying in time,
As whispers spin tales with a comical rhyme.

A chipmunk shares secrets, all wide-eyed and bright,
While twigs poke each other in sheer delight.
"Did you see the owl? He thinks he's so wise,"
But his disco moves? A surprise in disguise!

Fluttering butterflies join with a spin,
With colors that twirl like they're wearing a grin.
The forest becomes a hilarious show,
With nature's laughter, the stories will grow.

Amidst the chirps and the rustling leaves,
Every creature listens, no one believes.
The branches all sway, embracing the dance,
Here in the wild, everyone takes a chance.

Scribbled secrets of the wild

Bark bears stories, each scratch and line,
Tales of the critters who sip summer wine.
Mice write their memoirs with bits of a twig,
Expressing their lives, big dreams on a gig.

Bees buzz their ballads, sweet sticks of gold,
In recipes scribbled, their stories retold.
Each flower spins yarns of perfume and cheer,
As vines curl up close, leaning in to hear.

A raccoon pens poems on fallen old leaves,
Chasing his dreams in the bright summer eves.
With scratchy old quills, all letters are bright,
Cackling with laughter, they scribble 'til night.

The forest delights in its comical lore,
With secrets that sparkle on nature's grand floor.
Every whisper and wisp dances freely thus,
In the heart of the wild, there's laughter for us.

Echoes of the whispering pines

Pine cones drop echoes, thudding with fun,
As if nature's laughter is never quite done.
With shadows that tickle and branches that jest,
The whispers of pines hold the quirkiest quest.

Breeze plays the flute while the squirrels clap paws,
A raucous set filled with nature's own flaws.
"Did you hear that?" a fox points with glee,
"Those pines are the funniest friends, can't you see?"

The wind, like a jester, dances around,
Spinning tall tales with a whimsical sound.
Each rustling needle and creaking old trunk,
Echoes the laughter, never to funk.

The forest's alive with humor so bright,
Painting the pines in delightful twilight.
In the arms of the woods, the funny will stay,
Echos of joy, forever in play.

www.ingramcontent.com/pod-product-compliance
Lightning Source LLC
Chambersburg PA
CBHW072141200426
43209CB00051B/252